IMAGES
of America

ROUTE 66
IN ILLINOIS

This map of Route 66 in Illinois was issued by the Curve Inn, advertised as on Highway 66 at Main Street in Lemont. It was printed about the time Route 66 was moved from Route 4 through Auburn and Carlinville to the new alignment through Litchfield in 1933. By that year, however, Route 66 no longer ran through Lemont, and the Curve Inn was actually on Route 4A. (Authors' collection.)

ON THE COVER: The two longest paved highways in the world at the time met in Plainfield, the "Crossroads of America." The post-1940 alignment of Route 66 intersected the historic Lincoln Highway, US 30, directly in front of Sam Reichert's Standard station. The two legendary highways shared alignment for three blocks along present-day Illinois Route 59. (Courtesy of Route 66 Association of Illinois.)

IMAGES
of America

ROUTE 66
IN ILLINOIS

Joe Sonderman and Cheryl Eichar Jett

ARCADIA
PUBLISHING

Published by Arcadia Publishing
Charleston, South Carolina

Printed in the United States of America

Library of Congress Control Number: 2013954906

For all general information, please contact Arcadia Publishing:
Telephone 843-853-2070
Fax 843-853-0044
E-mail sales@arcadiapublishing.com
For customer service and orders:
Toll-Free 1-888-313-2665

Visit us on the Internet at www.arcadiapublishing.com

"May the road rise to meet you and its number be 66."
—Tom Teague

CONTENTS

ACKNOWLEDGMENTS

A special note of thanks is due to Cathie Stevanovich and the Route 66 Association of Illinois, who opened their doors and their exhibit cases to us on more than one occasion to scan photographs for many hours. We also owe special thanks to Route 66 collector extraordinaire Steve Rider and all of the other contributors listed in the photograph credits. We also wish to thank the following people for their assistance: Heather Bigeck, Marty Blitstein, Rich Dinkela, Josh Friedrich, Melinda Garvert, Anne Jackson, Curtis Mann, Randy Miller, Joseph Putnam, Sandy Vasko, and Mike Ward. Unless otherwise noted, all images are from the authors' collection.

INTRODUCTION

Illinois is where the road began, but it was a bumpy ride at first. At the turn of the 20th century, most long-distance travel was conducted by rail, and roads were afforded little importance. The black prairie soil turned into a quagmire when it rained, and wagon wheels often became solid cylinders of mud as wide as a bass drum. There were only 600 cars in the state, and roads were the responsibility of local townships. Each township had three commissioners, meaning there were 4,800 road officials! In 1910, Illinois began licensing vehicles with funds earmarked for roads. The Tice Act of 1913 approved state bonds for construction, shifted responsibility to the counties, and did away with all of those commissioners.

By this time, private associations were marking roads on their own. Much of Route 66 would follow the Pontiac Trail, named for the chief of the Ottawa tribe and marked in 1915 by the B.F. Goodrich Company. In 1916, the federal government authorized $75 million in road funds nationally over the next five years. The route between Chicago and St. Louis was one of five roads in Illinois to receive a share of those funds.

Also in 1916, the state laid out a plan for 4,000 miles of "hard roads" financed by a bond issue, which passed in 1918. State Bond Issue (SBI) Route 4 was assigned to the route from Forty-eighth Street and Ogden Avenue in Cicero to East St. Louis. Gov. Len Small won the 1920 election with a pledge to quickly complete the state road system. SBI 4 was paved along its entire length by the end of 1923, and Small pushed for a $100 million bond issue, which passed in 1924.

Businesses that once served the horse-and-buggy trade, such as stables and general stores, began selling gasoline from curbside pumps and performing repairs. Refining companies established stations along the highway. Automobile travelers often shunned the city hotels, preferring to camp by the roadside or in free tourist parks.

By the Roaring Twenties, traffic was on the increase. Rumrunners smuggled illegal hooch up and down Route 4, and the gang wars in Chicago and St. Louis spilled into the countryside. Meanwhile, overloaded trucks were destroying the roads. In 1921, lawmakers authorized the hiring of eight state highway patrol officers to cover all of Illinois. At first, their main concern was enforcing the weight limits.

In 1925, the federal government moved to eliminate the confusing patchwork of private and state routes. A committee assigned even numbers to the proposed east-west federal highways, with the most important ending in "0." The route between Chicago and Los Angeles was designated as "60," due mainly to the efforts of Cyrus Avery. A committee member from Tulsa, Oklahoma, Avery made sure the highway through his hometown was a continuous route and had an important-sounding number. But Kentucky governor William Fields demanded that "60" be assigned to the route through his state. After a battle of angry telegrams, Avery and his supporters agreed to accept the catchy-sounding "66" on April 30, 1926. The numbering system became official on November 11, 1926. Much of old SBI 4 became US Route 66. At that time, Illinois and Kansas were the only two states where Route 66 was completely paved, and Kansas could only claim 13 miles out of the entire route.

Avery coined the phrase "The Main Street of America," and the US 66 Highway Association set out to publicize the route. A footrace from Los Angeles to New York, dubbed the "Bunion Derby," provided the opportunity. A diverse group of 199 runners started from Los Angeles on March 4, 1928, and promoter C.C. "Cash and Carry" Pyle pledged a first prize of $25,000. The men ran in all sorts of conditions, with Pyle pinching pennies on accommodations and food. Just 72 men made it to East St. Louis on April 27. Near Staunton, eccentric runner and actor Lucien Frost was disqualified for riding in the trunk of a car. It cost him a movie deal. In Joliet, the runners cheered when creditors seized Pyle's lavish custom bus. In an effort to save money by forcing more runners to quit, Pyle increased the daily run to 59 miles. Another 12 men dropped out by the time the runners reached Chicago on May 5. A half-Cherokee named Andy Payne, from the Route 66 town of Foyil, Oklahoma, won the race, and Route 66 reaped the publicity.

Route 66 was evolving from the day it was commissioned. A new route was already under construction across the Des Plaines River from the old Pontiac Trail through Lemont and Lockport. The original route between Springfield and Staunton was bypassed in 1931 in favor of a straighter shot via Litchfield and Mount Olive.

During the Great Depression, images of desperate refugees from the Dust Bowl inspired John Steinbeck to label Route 66 "The Mother Road." But Route 66 brought economic opportunity to Illinois, as mom-and-pop cafés, gas stations, and motels sprang up and government relief programs put men to work improving the roads. In 1933, the terminus was moved from Cicero to the entrance to Grant Park at Jackson Boulevard in Chicago. In 1940, a new route opened through Plainfield and Gardner. The route through Joliet and Wilmington became Alternate 66.

The 1941 Defense Highway Act authorized construction of a modern four-lane, limited-access route between Chicago and St. Louis. During World War II, oversized trucks and heavy equipment left many sections virtually unusable. In some areas, plans called for two new lanes to be constructed and the old lanes abandoned. The abandoned lanes would be rebuilt after the war, creating a four-lane highway. New high-speed bypasses were constructed around most of the rural communities by 1946.

The postwar years are considered the golden age, when Nat King Cole sang "Get your kicks on Route 66" and Americans hit the road in record numbers. But the popularity of Route 66 also led to its demise, as the old two-lane sections became inadequate. Work continued on four-lane, limited-access segments from Glenarm to Raymond, completed in 1950, and between Braidwood and Gardner, which became Interstate 55 in 1956. In 1951, work began on the new highway south of Springfield. The four-lane route from Sherman to Lincoln opened in October 1953, and work began between Dwight and Chenoa in 1955. A new route between Staunton and Troy bypassed Edwardsville and Hamel. In October 1956, the new section between Worden and Troy virtually completed the four-lane highway between Chicago and St. Louis. Interstate 55 now follows most of the postwar four-lane route. The Route 66 shields came down in 1977.

But Route 66 is not dead. The old road is still there. Mom-and-pop motels still offer a chance to relax in one of their quirky rooms and drift off to sleep to the sweet sound of the highway. There are diners waiting with a counter stool and a cup of hot coffee. Attractions and photo opportunities line the route. Take a look at Illinois—where the road began!

One

COOK AND DUPAGE COUNTIES

Route 66 originally began at Jackson Boulevard and Michigan Avenue. In 1937, Jackson Boulevard and Route 66 were extended to the new Outer Drive, which became Lake Shore Boulevard in 1946. In 1953, Jackson was made one way, eastbound, west of Michigan. From Michigan to Lakeshore, Jackson continued to carry two-way traffic, as shown here. But westbound traffic had to turn north at Michigan and then west on Adams Street.

A grand building on Michigan Avenue was constructed for use during the 1893 Columbian Exposition, with the agreement that it would become the permanent home of the Art Institute of Chicago. The entrance is flanked by two bronze lions sculpted by Edward Kemys. A modern wing added in 2009 makes it the second-largest art museum in the United States.

In this view looking north from the intersection of State and Adams Streets in Chicago, the twin towers of Marina City can be seen in the background. Marina City is a mixed-use, residential-commercial complex completed in 1964 on the north bank of the Chicago River. The Route 66 alignments on Jackson Boulevard and Adams Street pass many other landmarks, such as the Railway Exchange Building, the Chicago Board of Trade, and Union Station.

Herman Joseph Berghoff opened a male-only saloon at State and Adams Streets in 1898. The Berghoff survived Prohibition by becoming a full-service restaurant and offering near beer and soda. It received Chicago liquor license no. 1 upon the repeal of Prohibition. The Berghoff remained off-limits to females until 1969. It is now operated by the fourth generation of the family.

In 1923, William Mitchell opened a restaurant on Jackson Boulevard, and his son Lou later took over. The restaurant later relocated to the other side of the street. Female patrons at Lou Mitchell's are still welcomed today with a box of Milk Duds candy. The tradition began as a symbol of Greek hospitality. The candy was originally made in Chicago by one of Lou's friends. (Courtesy of Route 66 Association of Illinois.)

Route 66 leaves the city of Chicago on Ogden Avenue, because it was the best route across a dismal nine-mile swamp, once an important Native American portage between Lake Michigan and the Des Plaines River but a serious impediment to the growth of Chicago. The road was named for Chicago's first mayor, William Butler Ogden, in 1872. The intersection of Ogden Avenue with Cermak and Pulaski Roads forms a triangle, as shown here.

Louis Ehrenberger built a service station resembling a castle next to his home on Ogden Avenue in 1925. He leased the station to John J. Murphy, who eventually bought the station and owned it until at least 1964. It became S & B Standard Service, and then was known as Gas Village. During the 1980s, it became the Castle Car Wash and was later abandoned. It is the last remaining historic service station on the Ogden Avenue portion of Route 66.

In 1904, Western Electric, the manufacturing arm of Bell Telephone, began transforming 113 acres of prairie into the massive Hawthorne Works. Over 45,000 people once worked at one of the largest manufacturing plants in the world. Research at the facility led to the high vacuum tube, sound motion pictures, radar, and the transistor. The plant closed in 1983, and the site became a shopping center. The tower is still there.

The Cindy Lyn Motel has been in business in Cicero since 1960. Management handed out free Zippo lighters to cabbies who brought passengers there. Just down Ogden Avenue, Bill Henry began selling hot dogs from a wooden trailer in 1946 and then built a redbrick building containing six stools. When a McDonald's opened nearby in 1960, Henry added a ceramic-tile exterior and designed a new sign. Customers still find that a hot dog from Henry's is "a meal in itself."

Ogden Avenue in Berwyn was once known as "Automobile Row," with 25 new- and used-car dealerships, including Suburban Nash (shown here). The dealership later became Suburban Dodge. Berwyn Kia opened at that location in 2011. Ogden Top and Trim, 6609 Ogden Avenue, is a notable survivor. It was founded in 1919 by Frank Nesladek and remains in the family. (Courtesy of Steve Rider.)

Joe (left), Andy (center), and Vincent Granatelli started out racing on tracks along Route 66 between Chicago, Springfield, and St. Louis, and they opened a performance parts store in Chicago. During the postwar housing shortage, they set a record for hauling mobile homes from Chicago to Los Angeles, often traveling over 100 miles per hour. Andy later gained fame in the Indianapolis 500 and helped make the STP fuel additive famous around the world. He was named to the Route 66 Association of Illinois Hall of Fame in 2003. Andy died on December 29, 2013. (Courtesy of Route 66 Association of Illinois.)

Hamburger restaurants had an unsavory reputation until Walter Anderson and Billy Ingram of Wichita, Kansas, started the first standardized chain in 1921. They chose a white porcelain castle design to symbolize purity and strength. A White Castle restaurant has occupied the corner of Ogden and Harlem Avenues since 1939, although the structure shown here has been replaced. (Courtesy of White Castle Collection.)

HOFFMAN TOWER AND DAM *Riverside, Ill.*

The pre-1928 alignment of Route 66 continued west on Ogden Avenue and crossed the Des Plaines River. The Hoffman Tower and dam was built in 1908 by brewer George Hoffman Jr. It was part of a recreational complex developed by his firm for the people of Lyons. After decades of neglect, restoration began in the 1980s. The tower is now part of the Village of Lyons logo. Past the tower, the original Route 66 jogged onto Lawndale Avenue to join the post-1928 route at Joliet Road.

AUTO
RIDE

MERRY
GO
ROUND

FAIRYLAND PARK -- 40th Street at Harlem Ave. -- LYONS, ILL.

The post-1928 route turns south briefly onto Harlem Avenue. The west side between Thirty-ninth and Fortieth Streets is now lined with retail stores and car dealerships, but it was once the site of a colorful gypsy camp. Richard W. Miller and his wife, Helen, opened Fairyland Park on the site in 1938. The much-loved amusement park was family owned until it closed in 1977.

Pedicone's
7729 W. 43rd St.
(U. S. 66)
Lyons, Illinois

Post-1928 Route 66 followed Forty-third Street (Joliet Road) entering Lyons, where Albert and Susan Pedicone's restaurant advertised "fine Italian viands and delicacies" and "Old World food in a New World setting." The restaurant was torched on New Year's Day 1963. A Cicero mob boss was questioned in connection with the fire, but no one was ever convicted.

The Whoopee Ride was a unique roadside attraction. It was sort of a roller coaster for automobiles, a wooden oblong track with dips and turns. Drivers paid 25¢ to take their own vehicles once around. It is visible in this photograph of Lorraine Spevacek Marek, taken on the roof of the adjacent Houdek's Restaurant, which was owned by her uncle. The Skyline Motel occupies the former site of the Whoopee Ride today. (Courtesy of Route 66 Association of Illinois.)

Joseph Houdek's Steak House was at the corner of Route 66 and Lawndale Avenue. Houdek's included a dance hall with a jukebox, a bar, and a soda fountain. There were living quarters on the second floor, with rooms for rent. Entertainers often spent the night. The building later became a 24-hour gas station, and it now houses a tire store.

Snuffy's Restaurant on Joliet Road was a Route 66 landmark from 1930 until 2010, when it was taken over by the Chicago-based Steak N Egger chain. Joliet limestone, quarried just up the road, was used for the exterior of the building. Sadly, the old-fashioned sign disappeared just before the restaurant changed hands.

During the 1930s and 1940s, 180 new locomotives rolled off the line every day at the 30-acre Electromotive plant in McCook. Electromotive became a full division of General Motors in 1941, and the plant at one time employed 14,000 people. But demand plunged in the 1980s, and locomotive production ceased in December 1992. The assembly plant was demolished in 2005. The world headquarters and engine plant remain. (Courtesy of Route 66 Association of Illinois.)

SUNNYSIDE MOTEL

U. S. RTS. 66 and 45 — LA GRANGE, ILL.

Zdenka and Stanley Lenoch operated the Sunnyside Motel. In 1974, Stanley acquired the adjacent golf property and constructed the William Tell Restaurant and Holiday Inn. The site was once a chicken ranch owned by the family of the legendary Marx Brothers. Groucho Marx joked that the farm did not do very well, because family members spent too much time watching Cubs games at Wrigley Field.

John Blackburn built the Wishing Well Motel at Route 66 and Brainard Avenue in 1941. Emil and Zora Vidas took over in 1958 and connected the 10 original cabins. Emil died in 1985, Zora passed away in 2004, and the Wishing Well was demolished in 2007. The wishing well from the courtyard and the sign were saved and are on display at the Route 66 Association of Illinois Hall of Fame and Museum in Pontiac.

Irv Kolarik ran a gas station and lunch counter in Willowbrook, but decided to focus solely on food. He was offered a fried chicken recipe by two local women, and Kolarik soon needed more room. In 1946, his Nationally Famous Chicken Basket moved into the former Club Roundup and Triangle Inn next door. To attract business in the winter, Kolarik flooded the roof of the restaurant and hired ice skaters. Dell Rhea and his wife, Grace, bought the restaurant in 1963. Their son Patrick took over in 1986.

In 1903, Martin Madden built a summer home, a one-tenth scale version of the White House, in Darien as a 25th-anniversary present for his wife, Josephine. He named it Castle Eden. Martin died in 1913, and the building later housed a restaurant. Purchased by the Carmelite Order in 1959, the home and estate are now the National Shrine of St. Therese and Carmelite Retreat Center. (Courtesy of Darien Historical Society.)

Two

Will and Grundy Counties

In 1940, a new route opened through Plainfield, and the original Joliet alignment became Alternate 66. The routes split at Welco Corners, where Montana Charlie Reid ran his truck stop. Reid worked as a cowboy and circus calliope player before he became chauffeur for an oil company executive and ended up owning the company. Interstate 55 killed off the truck stop, but Reid opened a quirky flea market in the mid-1960s. He died in 1982, but the giant plastic chickens he put in place still loom over the crowded flea market today. (Courtesy of Steve Rider.)

Stuyvesant Peabody made a fortune in coal mining and then decided he wanted a restaurant that would offer an "out-in-the-country experience" close to the big city. In the early 1920s, he opened the White Fence Farm Restaurant on Joliet Road at Romeoville on part of a 450-acre farm. Robert and Doris Hastert took over in 1954, and their son, Robert Jr., continues the tradition of "the world's greatest chicken" at the restaurant, which can accommodate 1,000 customers in 11 dining rooms.

Route 66 originally crossed the Des Plaines River at Summit and dropped south along the Illinois & Michigan Canal. The canal, completed in 1848, provided a link between the Great Lakes and the Gulf of Mexico. Shown here near Lockport, the waterway made Chicago the center of trade for the Midwest. Today, a 61-mile recreational trail follows the old canal towpath, and the former headquarters in Lockport is a museum. (Courtesy of Will County Historical Museum.)

As Route 66 was being transformed into a four-lane highway, distinctive new buildings were constructed for the Illinois State Police headquarters at Lockport, Pontiac, and Springfield. The structure shown here at Lockport still serves District Five today. The District Six headquarters at Pontiac had Art Moderne touches, such as curved corners and glass bricks. From the air, it resembles a pistol.

By 1930, Route 66 followed present-day Route 53, passing the Stateville Maximum Security Correctional Center at Crest Hill. It opened in 1925, and famous inmates included the notorious murderers Nathan Leopold and Richard Loeb, who killed teenager Robert "Bobby" Franks in 1924 for the "thrill." The US government tested malaria vaccines on prisoners at Stateville during World War II, and mass murderer John Wayne Gacy was executed there in 1994. Stateville is also known for its panopticon, a roundhouse with a guard tower in the middle surrounded by cells.

The Ruby Street Bridge carrying Route 66 over the Des Plaines River in Joliet opened in 1935 and is one of only three movable bridges on Route 66. The other two cross the South Branch of the Chicago River in Chicago. The bridge rotates on a large trunnion, or axle, to rise. It was reconstructed in 1972 and renovated in 2012. (Courtesy of Joliet Area Historical Museum.)

Early Route 66 passed the original Illinois State Penitentiary on Collins Street in Joliet. The prison was built in 1858 by convict labor. Its 25-foot-tall, five-foot-thick walls are made of pure Joliet limestone quarried on the site. It was closed in 2002. The classic prison architecture made it a perfect set for several movies and television productions, including the motion picture *The Blues Brothers*. (Courtesy of Joliet Area Historical Museum.)

J.F. "Grandpa" McCullough developed soft-serve ice cream, "frozen seconds before you eat it," and named the product Dairy Queen. On June 22, 1940, Sherb Noble opened the first Dairy Queen location at 501 North Chicago Street in Joliet. A soft-serve cone sold for a nickel. The building now serves as a Spanish-language church. (Courtesy of Joliet Area Historical Museum.)

Joliet was originally named Juliet, probably a corruption of the name of explorer Louis Jolliet. The name was changed in 1845. Route 66 originally followed Chicago Street, which later became one-way southbound; northbound traffic used Ottawa Street. In 1940, the route was moved to pass through Plainfield, and the Joliet route became Alternate 66. The alignment that became Interstate 55 opened in 1956. (Courtesy of Joliet Area Historical Museum.)

The Rialto Square Theatre is a beautiful mix of Greek, Roman, Baroque, and Byzantine styles, with a lobby modeled after the Hall of Mirrors at the Palace of Versailles outside Paris. "The Jewel of Joliet" opened on May 24, 1926, and was restored in 1980. It still hosts a variety of events and is said to be haunted by a couple of ghostly spirits. (Courtesy of Joliet Area Historical Museum.)

The Hotel Louis Joliet was the finest in the region during its heyday. The eight-story, 225-room hotel, built in 1927, was planned by the same developers who constructed the Rialto Square Theatre. It became a nursing home in 1964 and was remodeled into a performing arts center in 1980. It is now the Louis Joliet Apartments. (Courtesy of Joliet Area Historical Museum.)

The Woodruff Inn was located at Jefferson and Scott Streets. It opened on November 1, 1915, and was one of the first motels with fire sprinklers. It was demolished in 1971. This west-facing view was taken from the Union Depot in Joliet. In the background is the third Will County Courthouse, constructed in 1887 on the public square at Jefferson and Chicago Streets. It was razed in 1969.

Designed by architect Jarvis Hunt, Joliet's Union Depot was built in 1912. Renovation by the City of Joliet was completed in 1991. It still serves passengers, and the former passenger waiting area is now a private banquet hall. As of 2014, plans were in motion for a multimodal transportation center, which would move rail service from the station. (Courtesy of Joliet Area Historical Museum.)

Myron Fitzhenry operated the Fitzhenry Oil station at 76 South Chicago Street in Joliet. He is shown here during a World War II scrap tire drive. When Interstate 55 opened in 1956, Fitzhenry's business dropped by 75 percent. But the weigh scales he had installed kept him in business until his retirement. Paul Toth, who had worked at Fitzhenry's for 28 years, bought the station in 1988. He retired in 1998, and the site is now a parking lot. (Courtesy of Route 66 Association of Illinois.)

On the eve of World War II, the government assembled over 36,000 acres of land for the Elwood Ordnance Plant and the Kankakee Ordnance Works. Many of the nearby farms were acquired through eminent domain to create a huge buffer zone. Over one billion pounds of TNT and 926 million bombs and shells were made here during the war. The facilities were combined and re-designated as the Joliet Arsenal in 1945. (Courtesy of Joliet Area Historical Museum.)

This worker packing fuses was one of 10,000 people employed at the ammunition plants during World War II. A memorial honors 48 workers who died in an explosion at the Elwood Ordnance Plant on June 5, 1942. Most of the land is now the Abraham Lincoln National Cemetery, the second-largest national cemetery in the nation, and the Midewin National Tallgrass Prairie. The 19,000-acre prairie is the largest single area of open space in Illinois. (Courtesy of Joliet Area Historical Museum.)

Plainfield was known as the "Crossroads of America," because the two longest paved highways in the world at the time intersected there. The post-1940 alignment of Route 66 intersected the historic Lincoln Highway, US 30, directly in front of Sam Reichert's Standard station. The two legendary highways shared alignment for three blocks along present-day Illinois Route 59. (Courtesy of Joliet Area Historical Museum.)

Manor Motel - U. S. 6 and 66 - Joliet, Ill.

The Manor Motel at US Route 66 and US Route 6 originally had 13 rooms. Masonry contractor Walter Anderson built the first section in 1946. The motel was expanded four times over the years, to a total of 77 rooms. Leonard and Josephine Kowalski took over in the 1970s and sold it in 1999. Owner Prakash Silveri keeps the motel an attractive destination for Route 66 travelers today.

The Braceville Bridge over the Illinois River was the first steel-tied through arch bridge built in the state. This thoroughfare became Route 129 when Route 66 was moved onto the alignment to the west that became Interstate 55. A 1994 inspection showed that the bridge had been allowed to deteriorate, to the point that it was closed to traffic. After attempts to sell it failed, the bridge was demolished in 2000. (Courtesy of Library of Congress.)

Forrest and Bernice Gray's gas station and café opened on Route 66 at Braceville in 1923. It also served as the local Greyhound bus stop. The Standard Red Crown thermometer at right is now on display at the Route 66 Association of Illinois Hall of Fame and Museum in Pontiac, and Forrest and Bernice were inducted in 2004. (Courtesy of Route 66 Association of Illinois.)

In 1928, former miner James Girot combined a church building, a mine office, and even part of a school to create the Riviera Roadhouse. Al Capone is said to have been a frequent guest. The interior was a maze. The toilets sat atop a "throne" due to frequent floods, and the bar ceiling was decorated with papier-mâché stalactites. Bob and Peggy Kraft owned the Riviera for 37 years before retiring in 2008. This landmark on the Mazon River burned to the ground on June 8, 2010. (Courtesy of Route 66 Association of Illinois.)

Services for African American travelers were often hard to find, and many relied on Victor Green's *The Negro Motorist Green Book*, first published nationally in 1937. The guide could be found at Esso stations, one of the few chains to welcome African Americans. Green wrote, "There will be a day sometime in the future when this guide will not have to be published." He ceased publication after passage of the Civil Rights Act of 1964. This photograph was taken at Gardner, where Alternate 66 rejoined the post-1940 route. (Courtesy of Steve Rider.)

The historic two-cell Gardner jail was built in 1906. Closed in the 1950s, it has been restored and is a popular spot for photographs. Nearby is the Rev. Christian Christiansen Memorial, honoring the man who helped keep the Nazis from developing the atomic bomb during World War II. A Gardner church pastor, Christiansen worked with the US Navy to share his knowledge of the Nazi-held area of his native Norway.

This horse-drawn streetcar, once part of the Kankakee Transit System, was brought to Gardner to serve as a diner in 1932. George Kaldem was the owner; his mother, Minnie Springborn, was the cook and baker. The little streetcar was moved behind the Riviera in 1955 and was used for storage. Bob and Peggy Kraft donated the streetcar diner to Gardner after the 2010 fire that destroyed the Riviera, and it has been restored.

A green dinosaur, the symbol of Sinclair, stood watch on opening day in 1963 at Harold and Bob Stainbrook's station at Baltimore and Main Streets in Wilmington. The dinosaur was gone by the time Gary Geiss opened G&D Tire here in 2001. But one of the 80-pound fiberglass figures that once graced a Sinclair in Chattanooga, Tennessee, now stands on the roof, and Gary showcases a collection of Sinclair memorabilia inside. (Courtesy of Gary Geiss.)

Harry (left) and James (center) Butcher ran a garage and auto dealership in Wilmington. They finished 14th in the 1930 Indianapolis 500, with Harry behind the wheel and James as mechanic. Harry returned the following year, but crashed after a few laps and was badly hurt. In 1937, the brothers built the Mar Theater in Wilmington, which is still showing first-run movies. The dealership was later sold to the Lombardi family. (Courtesy of Gary Geiss.)

The Eagle Hotel in Wilmington (left) was built about 1838, and may be the oldest commercial structure on Route 66 in Illinois. It served as a boardinghouse, a bank, and a tavern before being converted to apartments in the 1940s. The storefronts were occupied until 1982, when the Wilmington Historical Society bought the structure. (Courtesy of Steve Rider.)

In 1965, owners John and Bernice Korelc changed the name of their Dari-Delite in Wilmington to the Launching Pad Drive-In. They purchased a 28-foot-tall fiberglass muffler man, turned him into an astronaut, and held a contest among the schoolchildren of Wilmington to pick a name. Cathy Thomas came up with Gemini Giant. He still greets travelers today, but the Launching Pad closed in 2013. (Courtesy of Route 66 Association of Illinois.)

In 1927, Peter Rossi and his brother John opened an elegant ballroom in a clearing they called Eagle Park and displayed a rescued crippled eagle in a cage. Rossi's Ballroom burned down in 1935, and Peter and John built the station shown here, with its white ceramic veneer, when Route 66 was realigned in 1939. In 1951, they added the Rossi Motel, now the Braidwood Motel. The station is now M & R Tire and Auto. (Courtesy of Route 66 Association of Illinois.)

The row of Rossi businesses in Braidwood also included a restaurant building leased to the Weitz brothers, Conrad and Frank. Their original café was located on Liberty Street in Morris, Illinois. Most of the food was prepared at Morris and brought to Braidwood in a little truck. The café faded when Braidwood was bypassed in 1956, and the building became a laundry establishment.

Effie Dornbierer (left) began waiting on tables at a diner on Route 66 at Odell in 1931, when she was just 14 years old. A few years later, she moved to Virgil's Café in Braidwood, where she met her future husband, Paul Marx (right). Effie Marx became the longest-working waitress on Route 66, serving for 60 years. She was named to the Illinois Route 66 Hall of Fame in 1993 and died in 1997. (Courtesy of Route 66 Association of Illinois.)

Three

LIVINGSTON COUNTY

Located at the "First Stoplight from Chicago," where Route 66 met Illinois Route 47 at Dwight, the Coffeehouse was part of a small chain. There were also locations on Route 66 at Bolingbrook and Pontiac. This location advertised "a friendly little restaurant featuring a hearty breakfast menu from 1:00 a.m. until 11:00 a.m., and a casual luncheon menu of freshly prepared top quality food the other 14 hours."

The Chicago & Alton Railroad depot at Dwight was built in 1891 and designed by Henry Ives Cobb. He also designed the first buildings at the University of Chicago, the Newberry Library, and the Chicago Post Office. This structure was renovated beginning in 1984 and now houses the Dwight Historical Society Museum and the chamber of commerce. Amtrak trains were still serving the station six times a day as of 2014. (Courtesy of Library of Congress.)

The First National Bank Building in Dwight, the building at center with the clock, was designed by Frank Lloyd Wright in 1905. The buildings on the right were Dr. Leslie Keeley's Institute, the first facility to treat alcoholism as a disease. The institute brought thousands of people to the once quiet railroad town. Dwight became a "model village," with paved streets and electric lights. The former institute is now the state's Fox Developmental Center.

Jack Schore opened a Texaco station in 1933, where Route 66 met Illinois Route 17 at Dwight. Basil "Tubby" Ambler added service bays and ran the station from 1938 until 1965. It changed hands a couple more times before Phil Becker took over in 1970. The station was later re-branded as Marathon. It was one of the longest-continually-operated stations on Route 66 before closing in 2002. Becker donated the station to the City of Dwight, and it is now a visitor's center.

Strufe Motel
Routes 66, 47 and 17 on Old 66
Dwight, Illinois

Just south of the Ambler station, Martin and Metha Paulsen operated Paulsen's Court and a service station from 1936 to 1950. The property was sold to John and Dorothy Strufe, who renamed it the Strufe Motel. In 1959, they converted the gas station into an office, the units were connected, and it became the Arrow Motel. The Strufes died in a 1968 automobile accident, and the Moyemont family changed the name to the Carefree Motel, now private residences.

A small lunch stand called Boyd's Place opened on Illinois Route 4 at Odell in 1925, a year before the road became Route 66. Boyd Fairchild and his brother Roy served food prepared in the kitchen of the family home. One night in the late 1930s, Boyd overheard two customers plotting to rob John Stonecipher's gas station across the highway. He sneaked out the back and alerted Stonecipher to close early. (Courtesy of Route 66 Association of Illinois.)

Dick Jones' Garage served travelers in Odell, where there was so much traffic on Route 66 that a pedestrian tunnel, or subway, was constructed in 1937. The subway allowed pedestrians to cross safely to St. Paul's Catholic Church and School. It became obsolete when the four-lane Route 66 bypassing Odell opened in 1944. In 1947, the tunnel was filled in and sealed with concrete. (Courtesy of Route 66 Association of Illinois.)

Patrick O'Connell constructed his station in Odell in 1932, using the "domestic style" design developed by Standard Oil. It later switched to Phillips 66 and then to Sinclair Gasoline. Robert Close bought the station in 1967 and operated a body shop until the Village of Odell bought it in 1999. The Route 66 Association of Illinois restored the station, which now serves as a visitor's center. (Courtesy of Route 66 Association of Illinois.)

Barns painted with advertisements for Meramec Caverns in Stanton, Missouri, were once a common site on Route 66. Caverns owner Lester Dill was a promotional genius who offered to have barns painted for free in return for the advertising space. The example shown here, restored by the Route 66 Association of Illinois Preservation Committee, is the last one remaining on the route in Illinois. A similar barn in Hamel was destroyed by a storm in 2011.

Joe Soda's Hilltop Café at Cayuga, with its unisex outhouse, was famous for hosting dances featuring local bands under the stars during the summer. The building once served as a schoolhouse. For a couple of years in the 1960s, it was operated by Joy and Archie Henderson, owners of Archie's Service Station in Pontiac. The building was later occupied by Sun Trucking. (Courtesy of Route 66 Association of Illinois.)

Joe and Victor "Babe" Seloti used cedar telephone poles to build the Log Cabin Inn lunchroom and gas station at Pontiac in 1926. Joe's pet crow conversed with customers and was fond of beer. When the new highway was constructed behind the Log Cabin in 1940, the Selotis used horses to turn the building around to face the new highway. The station was later converted to a private residence, but the café is still in business. (Courtesy of Route 66 Association of Illinois.)

G.I. Wetherholt's Ideal Cabin Court, the Ideal Service Station and Garage, and the Ideal Lunch Stand were located just south of the 1926 bridge over North Creek, where Route 66 originally curved into Pontiac. The camp included 10 octagon-shaped cabins and a garage that operated around the clock. The old bridge is still there, but the complex is gone. (Courtesy of Steve Rider.)

The Route 66 Association of Illinois Hall of Fame and Museum is located in the restored city hall and fire station in Pontiac. The city moved out of the building in 1986. In 2004, the hall of fame was relocated from the Dixie Trucker's Home to this historic building. In addition to its Route 66 exhibits and resources, the museum is now the home of the van and bus used by Route 66 artist and icon Bob Waldmire. (Courtesy of Steve Rider.)

Pontiac, founded as the county seat when Livingston County was created in 1837, is named after the great Ottawa Indian chief. In addition to its Route 66 attractions, Pontiac is notable for the Pontiac-Oakland Automobile Museum and for its three pedestrian swinging bridges across the Vermilion River. Harold "Pop" Lehmann operated the Cottage Café (shown here), next to city hall, for many years. During the 1930s, it served as the Atlantic & Pacific bus terminal.

The Livingston County Courthouse, on the square just off Route 66 in Pontiac, was built after a fire destroyed the previous one on July 4, 1874. Chicago architect John C. Cochrane designed it in Second Empire style, and a clock tower was installed in 1892. An Abraham Lincoln statue on the south side of the courthouse lawn commemorates the numerous visits Lincoln made to Pontiac during his lawyer days. (Courtesy of Library of Congress.)

Pericles "Pete" and Mary Petropoul's Liberty Café opened on the Pontiac square in 1919 after Pete returned from service in World War I. The International Walldog Mural and Sign Art Museum, dedicated to old-fashioned outdoor wall advertising, is located in this building. Artists who created such advertisements were known as "Walldogs," and a modern group of Walldogs has created many murals in Pontiac.

The Cozy Inn was operated by W.I. Lovenstein in the 1920s, before Illinois Route 4 became Route 66. Buses carrying passengers between Chicago and St. Louis often stopped here; the staff had 15 minutes to serve each busload. Mario's Pizza now occupies this building. The pizzeria is owned by Julie Causer and her husband. Julie's grandmother, Grace Lauritzen, was a waitress at the Cozy Inn in the 1930s. (Courtesy of Steve Rider.)

The Palamar on the original Route 66 (Ladd Street) was operated by Hal Halverson. It opened around 1940 and burned down in 1967. The new Palamar Inn was operated for many years by Jerry and Sara Hillyer. The motel had 62 units, and the restaurant was one of the finest in the area. The bar downstairs, known as the Pirate's Cove, included a real ship's hull. The Palamar was barely standing as of 2014.

The Fiesta Motel still stands on the northeast corner of four-lane Route 66 and Illinois Route 116. The bowling alley is one of several Pontiac locations featured in the 1984 movie *Grandview, U.S.A.*, starring Jamie Lee Curtis and Patrick Swayze. Part of a 2012 episode of the television series *Revolution* is set in Pontiac and features actor C. Thomas Howell. He was also a cast member of *Grandview, U.S.A.*

Archie and Joy Henderson operated Archie's Standard Service in Pontiac, "The Best Friend Your Car Ever Had." It was advertised as at the "second stoplight from Chicago," Route 66 and Illinois Route 116. The station would later be owned by Dick and Bev Harder and would become S&R Auto Repair. (Courtesy of Route 66 Association of Illinois.)

Rodino Square, on the southeast corner of Reynolds and Ladd Streets, was operated by the Carmen Rodino family beginning in 1927. It included a store, hotel, restaurant, and gas station. Carmen also sold produce grown by the family, making the rounds in his 1921 Model T truck. He continued to make deliveries into the 1960s. Rodino Square is gone, but it lives on in one of the Walldog murals on Main Street in Pontiac. (Courtesy of Route 66 Association of Illinois.)

Chester Henry patrolled Route 66 out of District Six Headquarters in Pontiac from 1957 until 1975. He then worked as an administrator until he retired in 1984. Henry once wrote 283 tickets in a single month, and he pulled over many celebrities and politicians. Trooper Henry was inducted into the Route 66 Association of Illinois Hall of Fame in 1993. (Courtesy of Route 66 Association of Illinois.)

Leroy Curtiss ran this Sinclair station, across Route 66 from the Illinois State Police District Headquarters. In 1949, Leroy and his wife, Pauline, opened the Curtiss Drive-In one block away. They later purchased Fred's Drive-In and turned it into Leroy's, known for its Dagwood Burger. From 1969 to 1975, they ran Pauline's Chicken Villa. Pauline and Leroy were later honored as the "King and Queen of the Drive-Ins" in Pontiac. Leroy is seen here standing in the doorway. (Courtesy of Route 66 Association of Illinois.)

Four

McLean County

Individual
Metal Showers
Toilets
Lavatories

Hot and Cold
Running Water

Innerspring
Mattresses
on All Beds

Plenty of Shade
Kool and Quiet

Butane Gas
Heated
for Winter

PEARSON'S MODERN CABINS
ON U. S. 66 — 4 BLOCKS NORTH OF U. S. 24
PHONE 101-R-2   CHENOA, ILLINOIS

Chenoa attracted early automobile travelers with a free camping spot in the city's Tourist Park. A lunchroom and gas station were built there in 1921, and Lloyd Sarver took over in 1926. Sarver added a few cabins, reportedly using converted chicken coops. Elvin Pearson later took over and then ran Pearson's Modern Cabins here until 1953. The site is now Redbird Park.

Chenoa was laid out in 1854 at the future junction of the Toledo, Peoria & Western Railway and the Chicago & Alton Railroad. Founder Mathew Scott called it "Chenowa," which he said was an American Indian name for his home state of Kentucky. The post office, however, recorded the name as Chenoa. The view in this photograph looks north from the intersection of Illinois Routes 4 and 8, later US Routes 66 and 24. (Courtesy of Steve Rider.)

Within just a few years, several businesses serving automobile travelers were located at the intersection that became US 66 and US 24. This route became City 66 when the four-lane highway was constructed in 1946. The four-lane alignment originally crossed the railroad tracks at grade level, resulting in harrowing traffic jams. Steve's Café is visible at right center, and the structure that housed the Sweney station (left) is still recognizable today.

Chenoa Motel   U.S. 66 & 24   Chenoa, Illinois

16 MODERN, STEAM HEATED UNITS
FIRST CLASS, 24 HOUR CAFE CLOSE
BY, RAY & GRACE ANDERSON, PROPS.

In 1948, Isaac Weaver built the first truly modern motel at Chenoa, an eight-unit complex near the intersection of four-lane US 66 and US 24. Ray Anderson took over the Chenoa Motel in 1950 and enlarged it to 16 units. It was later operated by his son and then was purchased by Murphy and Fiore of Chicago in 1952. The motel no longer stands.

"The Finest Steaks Between Chicago and St. Louis"

AIR CONDITIONED
STEVE'S CAFE

TEXACO

STEVE'S CAFE INTERSECTION CITY 66 & 24   CHENOA, ILLINOIS

The Wahls brothers opened their café at Chenoa in 1918. Their chef, Steve Wilcox, took over in the 1930s. Steve's was the first air-conditioned restaurant on Route 66 in Illinois outside of Chicago. Ken and Peg Stipe bought Steve's in 1975, and it became the Red Bird Lounge, which closed in 1997. The building still stands.

Schuirmann's Drug Store in Chenoa was founded in 1888 by Tido "Carl" Schuirmann and Henry Hops. Hops sold his share in 1909, and Carl's daughter Emma and her husband took over when he died in 1930. The building now houses the Chenoa Pharmacy, operated by Dan Boian. The original wood flooring and much of the original cabinetry remain at this historic business. (Courtesy of Route 66 Association of Illinois.)

A restored neon arrow sign points the way to Lexington, where Leo Bornder (shown here) ran his station from 1948 until 1989. Maggie Giles and her daughter Cricket ran the restaurant, and local lore says Elvis Presley stopped here one night. Leo rebuilt after a 1960 fire and converted the station to self-service after Interstate 55 opened. But he let regular customers know that they could pull up to the inside set of pumps and get full service for the self-serve price. (Courtesy of Route 66 Association of Illinois.)

Carl Christianson and his son Richard opened the Lexington Motel at Route 66 and Main Street in 1950. Allen Gleeson's Mobil station was located next door. The motel was later owned by Harold and Mary Montgomery. The station was torn down after the construction of Interstate 55, but the motel was converted to apartments and still stands.

The Mesa Café, where "good food is served with prompt service," was built in the 1940s. It also served as a Skelly station. Located across from the Lexington Motel, it closed in the 1970s, and Jarrii Risberg bought the property in 1982, expanded the complex, and opened the Filling Station Restaurant. The restaurant later became Outback Pizza, now closed.

Sandwiched between the original Route 66 and the later four-lane alignment, the Oasis Drive In was a popular hangout on the southwest side of Lexington. From 1960 until 1976, it was operated by Elmo and Arline Winterland. The Oasis closed in the 1980s, and the Lexington High School History Club helped get the drive-in named to the Route 66 Association of Illinois Hall of Fame in 1998. The vacant drive-in and its battered sign still stand. (Courtesy of Route 66 Association of Illinois.)

Stuckey's stores, with their pitched roofs and teal blue shingles, were once a common sight. Locations on Route 66 in Illinois included one at Raymond and this one, a few miles south of Lexington. William S. Stuckey Sr. started out selling pecan candy at his stand in Georgia in the 1930s. The chain, known for its pecan log roll, had 350 locations during its heyday. Stuckey's faded after Pet Milk took it over in the 1970s, but it has been revived by W.S. Stuckey Jr.

In the summer of 1965, two strange-looking buildings rose along Route 66 north of Towanda. A house and granary, hand-carved by natives of the Luzon Mountain Province in the Philippines, served as a billboard for Asian Arts Associates, a shop selling Asian arts and crafts. Richard Long used the profits to found an agricultural cooperative for the natives.

The Delco Truck Stop opened at Towanda on June 29, 1952, and was originally operated by Del Haines. Three years later, it became the Pure Oil Truck Stop. Eddie Baize and his wife, Marjorie, became the owners in 1963, and the name was changed to Eddie's Pure/Union 76 Truck Stop. It closed after Interstate 55 opened in 1976. Directly behind the truck stop in this photograph is a section of Illinois 4/original Route 66 that earned the nickname "Dead Man's Curve." It was bypassed after World War II.

Fern and Mac McCurdie opened Fern's Café and Texaco in 1951, after Route 66 was expanded to four lanes in Towanda. The restaurant seated about 30 people. Mac and Fern were killed in an automobile accident in 1955, and Mac's brother Jack took over. He ran the restaurant until 1967. It closed in 1969, and the gas station was lost to Interstate 55 in 1977. (Courtesy of Towanda Area Historical Society.)

Route 66 originally followed several streets through Normal, including Pine, Linden, Willow, Main, and Kingsley Streets. The Diamond Camp, on Pine Street near Beech Street, got much of its business from visitors to the Illinois Soldiers' and Sailors' Children School, the state-run orphanage nearby. The Diamond Camp later became Manning's Tourist Village, which was in business into the 1960s. The site is now a trailer park. (Courtesy of Steve Rider.)

William Sprague's Super Service Station included a restaurant on the ground floor and apartments for the owner and station attendant on the second level. The Tudor Revival structure was built in 1931 and also housed Sprague's contracting business. The pumps were removed in 1979, and it became a bridal store, cake shop, and catering business. Current owner Terri Ryburn hopes to turn it into a Route 66 welcome station.

In 1899, Nancy Mason donated her home in Normal to the Methodist Episcopal Deaconess Society, for use as a home for both active and retired deaconesses. They were women who were trained as nurses, educators, evangelists, social workers, and administrators for mission work. The Baby Fold still serves at-risk children today, through adoption services, residential care, and special education and family services. (Courtesy of McLean County Museum of History.)

The state set up a teacher's college at North Bloomington in 1857, a time when teacher colleges were known as normal schools. The town was incorporated as Normal in 1856. Old Main, the first major building on campus, was completed in 1861. The school became Illinois State University at Normal in 1964, and then Illinois State University in 1968.

Gus Belt's Shell Inn Restaurant and gas station in Normal was struggling until he turned it into the White House Steak and Shake in 1934. Gus adopted the slogan "In Sight it Must be Right," because the beef was ground in front of the customers. Franchising began in 1945. The original location at Main Street and Virginia Avenue (shown here) was sold to Monical's Pizza in the 1990s. (Courtesy of McLean County Museum of History.)

Eldon "Casey" Casebeer took over a fruit stand at North Main and Kelsey Streets in Bloomington in 1949. It grew into Casey's Market Basket, the area's first 24-7 grocery store. After customers admired the rose bushes in front of the store, Casey began selling them at a seasonal garden shop in back. In 1968, he sold the grocery to run the garden shop year-round. His son-in-law Ray Lartz still operates Casey's Garden Shop and Florist. (Courtesy of Route 66 Association of Illinois.)

Quinn's station served motorists for over 70 years at Main and Chestnut Streets in Bloomington. It was established by twin brothers Elmo C. (top, left) and Eldon Quinn (top, right). Elmo A. Quinn began working for his father and uncle at the station in 1978. He provided customers with full service until retiring in December 2013. (Courtesy of Route 66 Association of Illinois.)

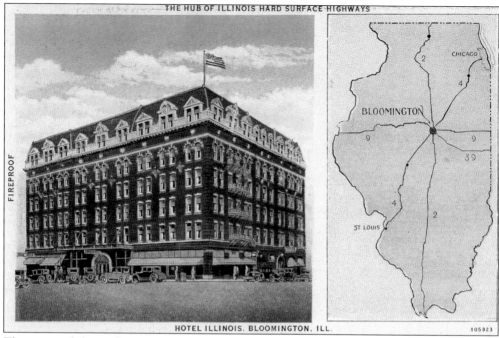

THE HUB OF ILLINOIS HARD SURFACE HIGHWAYS

HOTEL ILLINOIS, BLOOMINGTON, ILL.

This postcard shows the system of paved state highways in place across Illinois before Route 66 was commissioned. The Hotel Illinois was the most luxurious in Bloomington. It replaced the Hotel Windsor, which burned down in the 1900 fire that nearly wiped out downtown. The hotel was restored in 1977 and became the Illinois House, a premiere office space.

State Farm Insurance, founded by George J. Mecherle in 1922, originally specialized in automobile insurance for farmers. The firm moved into new headquarters in downtown Bloomington in 1929. The company rapidly outgrew the building, and four more stories and a penthouse were added in 1934. Additions in 1940 and 1945 brought the building to its present height. (Courtesy of McLean County Museum of History.)

Employees on roller skates sped delivery of mail and documents at the State Farm Insurance home office in the 1940s. The company supplied the skates, but employees were allowed to bring their own as long as they had rubber wheels. A new headquarters campus for State Farm was constructed on Veterans Parkway beginning in 1972. (Courtesy of Route 66 Association of Illinois.)

A site at the "Blooming Grove" was chosen for the county seat when McLean County was created in 1830. The old courthouse, built in 1900, now houses the McLean County Museum of History. Bloomington was the home of Jesse Fell, who convinced Abraham Lincoln to run for president, and Adlai Stevenson II, who ran for president twice and then served as US ambassador to the United Nations during the height of the Cold War. (Courtesy of Library of Congress.)

Italian immigrant George Ventura opened Ventura's Grill about 1950 at 1415 South Main Street. For several years, the family also lived in the building. Son George Jr. eventually became the manager, and son David became the cook, as George Sr. returned to one of his former jobs as a truck driver. In recent years, the building housed the South Hill Neighborhood Café, a Tex-Mex bakery, and a thrift store. (Courtesy of Steve Rider.)

Robert Dale "Bob" Johnson owned a restaurant on Main Street before taking over the Brandtville Café, on the southwest corner of Route 66 and US 150. He ran this restaurant for 35 years. It was open around the clock, and singer Bobby Darin made the news when he stopped here in 1963. This building was later replaced by a new structure with a big chicken on the roof that housed several restaurants over the years.

Paul Streid's restaurant, motel, and service station were located on the northwest corner of the 1941 Route 66 Belt Line (Veterans Parkway) and US 150. The motel had 32 units, and the service station was open around the clock. Streid's burned down on August 1, 1980. Streid was a civic leader who also owned the Saddle Club in downtown Bloomington and the Halfway House Restaurant, also on the Route 66 Belt Line.

Bloomington's only drive-in theater opened in 1947 at US 51 and the 66 Belt Line. The Phil-Kron, later the Bloomington Drive-In, was built by Ken Phillips and restaurateur Pete Karonis. The restaurant under the big screen was named the Phil-Kron Grill and later became the Country Kitchen. In December 1958, it became the Sinorak Smorgasbord ("Karonis" spelled backwards). The restaurant closed in 1980, and the drive-in burned down in September 1984.

Completed in December 1941, the Route 66 bypass around Bloomington and Normal was considered an engineering marvel. The four-lane, limited-access "Belt Line" was inspired by the autobahns of Germany, which were reportedly designed for speeds of up to 100 miles per hour. This bus has just exited the Belt Line and is turning north onto US 51 (Main Street). The Belt Line was renamed Veterans Parkway in 1979. (Courtesy of Illinois Department of Transportation.)

The 14-unit Rusk Haven Motel, operated by Stanley J. Lucas, was located on the southern edge of Bloomington. It stood just west of the junction with US 51 (Main Street) and across the Belt Line (now Veterans Parkway) from Highland Park Golf Course. It was advertised as being "on the hill next to Heaven." Part of the land was taken for construction of the ramp from Veterans Parkway to Main Street.

Maple syrup has been produced at Funks Grove since Isaac Funk arrived in 1824. His grandson Arthur began commercial production in 1891. Hazel Funk Holmes took over in the 1920s, after the "hard road" cut through their land and brought more customers. A trust she established protects the land and ensures the product will always be called "sirup," the correct term for the pure sap with no added sugar. Mike and Debby Funk continue the tradition today. (Courtesy of Mike and Debby Funk.)

General store operator J.P. Walters and his son-in-law opened gas stations in Shirley and McLean, and they started delivering their own product, Dixie Gas. They opened the Dixie Trucker's Home at Route 66 and US 136 in McLean on January 1, 1928. Walters, originally from Kentucky, said that the name Dixie symbolized Southern hospitality. Some of the staff pose for a photograph about 1940. They are, from left to right, Estelle Spaulding, Florence Hafley, Blanche Baumgardner, Bill Norbits, Buella Criswell, Eulla Mason, and Lorena Criswell.

The Dixie was open continuously until a fire on June 28, 1965. Within hours, the gas pumps were in operation, and one of the eight cabins on the property was moved up front to house the operation. A new building accommodating 250 people at a time opened in 1967. The business passed to John Geske's daughter and son-in-law, Charlotte and Chuck Beeler. (Courtesy of Route 66 Association of Illinois.)

Charlotte and Chuck Beeler made the Dixie one of the best-known truck stops on any highway, before selling to a corporation in 2003. The Route 66 Association of Illinois Hall of Fame was located in a hallway here until 2004, when it was moved to the museum in Pontiac. The landmark became the Dixie Travel Plaza, and it received a major renovation in 2009. The Road Ranger chain took over the Dixie in 2012.

Five

LOGAN COUNTY

Old 66 becomes Arch Street and curves into Atlanta, past the former site of Jim Brown's Restaurant and Texaco station (shown here). The building later became a church and was demolished in 1954. The community was originally called Xenia, but the name had already been claimed by another Illinois town. It was named after Atlanta, Georgia, in 1855. (Courtesy of Atlanta Museum.)

The octagonal Atlanta Public Library was dedicated in March 1908. Designer Paul Moratz of Bloomington combined a Neoclassical style with an unusual geometric shape. In 1982, a tower was completed on the grounds to house the 1909 Seth Thomas clock from the demolished Atlanta High School. The clock must be cranked by hand every eight days. (Courtesy of Atlanta Museum.)

The J.H. Hawes grain elevator, an Atlanta landmark, was built in 1904. The 60-foot-tall elevator, constructed of wood, utilized a vertical conveyor system to load grain into railcars bound for markets such as Peoria and Decatur. Abandoned in 1976, the elevator was saved from demolition by a group of local residents. The restored J.H. Hawes Grain Elevator is now a working museum, listed in the National Register of Historic Places.

James Robert Adams, inspired by palm trees he saw in California, opened the Palms Grill Café at Atlanta in August 1934. A light at the bottom of the sign signaled Greyhound bus drivers to stop for passengers. The cafe closed in the late 1960s, but it was restored in 2009. It occupies half of the Downey Building, which was constructed in 1867. (Courtesy of Atlanta Museum.)

Atlanta now boasts one of the most attractive streetscapes on the route. Across from the Palms Grill, a fiberglass muffler man holds a giant hot dog. The fiberglass giants were usually used to promote muffler or tire stores in the 1960s, but "Tall Paul" ended up at Bunyon's hot dogs in Cicero. He was brought to Atlanta and restored in 2003.

The photograph at top shows Illinois Route 4 from the top of the grain elevator between Lawndale and Lincoln. The image was taken in 1924, by which time Route 4 had been completely paved between Chicago and St. Louis. The bottom photograph was taken in 1944, when the four-lane Route 66 was completed. This segment was bypassed by Interstate 55. (Courtesy of Illinois Department of Transportation.)

Abraham Lincoln argued cases at the courthouse in Postville, now Lincoln. The building became a residence after the county seat was moved to Mount Pulaski in 1847. No one stepped forward to save it when the owner sold the historic structure to automaker Henry Ford in 1929. Ford had it dismantled and shipped for reassembly at his Greenfield Village Museum in Dearborn, Michigan. The state constructed a replica of the original courthouse at Lincoln (shown here) beginning in 1953.

Erected in 1903, the Logan County Courthouse is the third to stand on the square in Lincoln. Abraham Lincoln practiced law in the previous structure on the site, and he served as presiding judge of the Logan County Circuit Court in March 1859. The structure is considered the second-most architecturally significant historic courthouse in Illinois, after the Macoupin County Courthouse in Carlinville.

Dedication ceremonies were held in Lincoln on November 27, 1923, for Illinois Route 4. Speakers hailed the "Illini Route" as the "greatest highway in the world." A parade depicted transportation in Illinois from the Indian pony travois (shown here) to aircraft and modern automobiles. Gov. Len Small made a speech promoting a proposed $100 million bond issue that he said would build a hard road into every county seat in the state.

"Coonhound Johnny" Schwenoha was a bootlegger and hunting buddy of Al Capone who ran a roadhouse on Route 66 north of Lincoln. His son Vince spent time in Hawaii while in the service and opened the Tropics in 1950. It became known for a two-patty hamburger, which Schwenoha had seen in California. Lewis Johnson made the Tropics a center of the community during his ownership from the 1950s to 1997. The Tropics closed in 2005, but the sign and building still stand.

A curve on the four-lane bypass around Lincoln, completed in 1944, was one of the deadliest spots on the highway in Illinois. Drivers mostly ignored the posted speed limit of 45 miles per hour on the Blu-Inn Curve, named after the nearby restaurant (shown here). The Blu-Inn opened in 1953 across from the Tropics. In 1963, Bev and Lou Johnson changed the name to the Heritage Inn. The building no longer stands.

Wilfred "Squeak" Werth opened his Standard station at Lincoln in 1934. He claimed that it was the first in the state with modern pumps that added up the sale. Wilfred and his wife, Dorothy, opened the Redwood Motel here in 1956. They sold the motel to Ruth Buckles in 1963, and the station closed in 1993. The motel sign was replaced in 2000, and Sherman West and his wife, Joan, took over in 2003.

Lincoln is the only town named for the nation's 16th president while he was still alive. Abe Lincoln provided legal assistance during the founding of the community. Legend says that, on August 29, 1853, Lincoln used watermelon juice to christen the town and advised against naming it in his honor. He supposedly said, "You'd better not do that, for I never knew anything named Lincoln that amounted to much." The intersection of Illinois 10 and Beltline 66 (shown here) was known as the "Four Corners." (Courtesy of Illinois Department of Transportation.)

Waitresses, dressed in blue with white aprons, greeted the first customers at the Blue Mill in Lincoln on July 25, 1929. Paul Coddington's windmill-themed sandwich shop was painted blue with white trim. Albert and Blossom Huffman took over in 1945, painted it burgundy, and added a war surplus barracks to serve as a dance hall and barroom. Once famous for its schnitzel, the Mill closed in 1996. The Route 66 Heritage Foundation of Logan County has begun restoration.

One day in 1937, a customer at the Harbor Inn in Broadwell asked proprietor Ernie Edwards for a slice of "that pig hip," and a Route 66 landmark was born. Edwards changed the name to the Pig Hip and ran the restaurant until 1991, when it was turned into a museum. Ernie's sister built cabins next door, which were later enclosed as the Pioneer's Rest Motel. Fire destroyed the Pig Hip on March 5, 2007, and Ernie Edwards, the beloved "Old Coot," passed away in 2012.

Six

SANGAMON COUNTY

An April 1958 aerial photograph of Williamsville shows how Route 66 typically expanded and bypassed many rural communities in Illinois. Original Route 66 (Elm Street) ran through the heart of the village. The light-colored highway at left is the two-lane bypass constructed in 1940. In 1953, two additional lanes, appearing darker in the photograph, were added to complete the four-lane highway around the town. Interstate 55 bypassed it all in 1977.

The village of Williamsville was originally platted as Benton in 1853 and grew around the railroad stop. The Williamsville Museum, established in 1989, is located in two converted Gulf, Mobile & Ohio Railroad boxcars donated by a local resident. Next door, the historic train depot houses the Williamsville Library. Both are located on Elm Street alongside the Norfolk & Western Railroad tracks. (Courtesy of Williamsville Museum.)

Wilbur Fawns Sr. was a mechanic at Charles Sutton's Garage on Main Street in Williamsville and took over when Charles enlisted in the Army Air Forces in 1943. In 1954, Wilbur (shown here) bought Frank Fink's Standard. Wilbur and his sons, Wilbur Jr. and George, would go on to operate several stations in Williamsville and Sherman. Wilbur's wife, Ruth, operated the Route 66 Café just east of the Williamsville Standard Station from 1960 to 1984. (Courtesy of Wilbur Fawns Jr.)

Route 66 through Sherman originally followed today's Illinois Route 124 and then turned south on Old Tipton School Road to the Sangamon River. Visible today in Carpenter Park are two short segments of pavement dating back to 1922. Wood's Place was operated by Vernon Woods and his wife, Nora. Ruby Fishback took over in 1938 and opened the Hide-A-Way, which became a popular hangout for the youths of Sherman. (Courtesy of Donna Catlin.)

At his inaugural address in January 1953, Gov. William Stratton said he wanted four-lane Route 66 to be completed between Lincoln and Springfield in time for the Illinois State Fair in August. But chief highway engineer Frank N. Barker said it could not be done. The highway was built under a new chief engineer, but it still missed the governor's deadline. Governor Stratton, seen here at the microphone, dedicated the highway at Sherman on October 2, 1953. (Courtesy of Donna Catlin.)

In this photograph, with a view looking north toward Carpenter Park, a federal bus crosses the Sangamon River on Illinois Route 4 in February 1924. A four-lane bridge replaced the old iron bridge in 1936. Entering Springfield, original Route 66 turned onto Taintor Road on the north side of the state fairgrounds, and then followed North Fifth Street to turn west at North Grand Avenue before jogging south on Second Street past the capitol. (Courtesy of Sangamon Valley Collection, Lincoln Library.)

The Illinois State Fairgrounds, shown here in 1925, are on the north side of Springfield. The view in this photograph looks northwest, showing Peoria Road at the right, which later carried Route 66. At the far left is the beautiful Main Gate, constructed in 1910, with the fair's Main Street leading to the huge Exposition Building. The racetrack and grandstand were reconstructed two years after this photograph was taken. The so-called Springfield Mile is known as one of the fastest dirt tracks in the world.

Shown here is opening day at Jim Culver's Sinclair station at 101 South Second Street, on the 1926–1930 alignment. Motorists are being served by four attendants, and a mobile cash register has been set up. The station no longer stands, and the site is now a parking lot. Gietl Brothers Auto Body is visible in the background. The firm was established in 1904, and it is still in business at the same location. (Courtesy of Sangamon Valley Collection, Lincoln Library.)

Springfield was originally named Calhoun, in honor of Secretary of War John C. Calhoun of South Carolina. When Calhoun became vice president, his fiery speeches in favor of slavery spurred residents to rename their city. The name was changed in 1832, and the state capital was moved from Vandalia in 1837. The move was due partly to the efforts of a young politician named Abraham Lincoln. The sixth Illinois capitol (shown here) took 20 years to construct and is 74 feet taller than the US Capitol.

The 1926–1930 alignment passed Sweney's Service on Second Street, across from the capitol. The station became John Gray's DX in the late 1950s, but it no longer stands. The original route turned west onto South Grand Avenue and then south onto West Grand, now MacArthur Boulevard, curving onto present-day Wabash Avenue and entering Jerome. (Courtesy of Sangamon Valley Collection, Lincoln Library.)

This photograph was taken at Sixth and Jefferson Streets in downtown Springfield before Route 4 became Route 66. At left center, the overhang from Union Station is visible. The Firestone dealer at right is Delbert H. Gunnette's Tire and Vulcanizing store at 200 North Sixth Street. Route 10 eventually became US 36 and Interstate 72 to Riverton and Decatur. (Courtesy of Illinois Department of Transportation.)

Abraham Lincoln argued cases before the Illinois Supreme Court and served in the legislature in the Old State Capitol (center). Lincoln also delivered his famous "House Divided" speech here. It served as the capitol from 1840 until 1876 and as the Sangamon County Courthouse from 1876 to 1966. The structure was taken down stone by stone and completely reconstructed in the 1960s. (Courtesy of Sangamon Valley Collection, Lincoln Library.)

Maldaner's Restaurant is on the right in this 1947 photograph of traffic-clogged Sixth Street between Monroe and Adams Streets. Maldaner's is the oldest and most famous restaurant in Springfield, established by John Maldaner in 1884 and located in this building since 1894. The beautiful décor has changed very little since Walter Tabor renovated the restaurant in 1937. (Courtesy of Sangamon Valley Collection, Lincoln Library.)

The Leland Hotel (right), at Sixth Street and Capitol Avenue, is said to be the birthplace of the horseshoe sandwich, created by chef Steve Tomko in 1928. The Springfield specialty consists of Texas toast, hamburger or other meats, and French fries. It is all topped off with cheese sauce. The Hotel Abraham Lincoln (left), at Fifth Street and Capitol Avenue, opened in 1925. The once luxurious hotel was demolished in 1978. (Courtesy of Sangamon Valley Collection, Lincoln Library.)

During the Great Depression, 200 unemployed men of Springfield welcomed a plan by Firestone to put money in their pockets by giving them coupon books to sell. Firestone was celebrating the opening of this service center at 415 South Sixth Street in March 1932. This location is still in business today, and the building looks much the same. (Courtesy of Sangamon Valley Collection, Lincoln Library.)

In 1930, Route 66 was shifted to enter Springfield on Peoria Road on the east side of the fairgrounds, past the used-car lot owned by Jim Kelty and Alex Kish. The route then followed Ninth Street and jogged over to Sixth Street south of downtown. This alignment became City 66 in 1940, when a bypass opened following Thirty-first Street (now Dirksen Parkway) and Linn Avenue (now Adlai Stevenson Drive). The car in the foreground is a customized 1949 Ford convertible. (Courtesy of Sangamon Valley Collection, Lincoln Library.)

West of the intersection of City 66 (Peoria Road) and Bypass 66 (Thirty-first Street, now Dirksen Parkway) stood Little Chum's Lodge and the Pioneer Motel. Both motels were constructed in 1951, Little Chum's with 14 units and the L-shaped Pioneer with a dozen units. The 1958 Springfield city directory lists 34 motels on alignments of Route 66 in Springfield. The majority of them were built in the 1950s. Both of these buildings and the radio-style tower still stand. (Courtesy of Illinois Department of Transportation.)

This view of the west side of City 66, just south of the intersection with Bypass 66, shows Poland's Haven Motel, opened by Roy and Alice Poland in 1939, and the Capitol Motel. Little Chum's, the Pioneer, Poland's, and the Capitol were all in a row on the west side of City 66. The Capitol claimed to be the "North's finest." This site is now the North Oaks Mobile Home Park. (Courtesy of Illinois Department of Transportation.)

The Lazy A Motel at 2840 Peoria Road was built in 1949 by Harold Gordon and Daisy Gordon Tucker and exhibited a style of architecture usually found in the Southwest. It is the last example of a motor court with garages between the units on Route 66 in Illinois. Old wagon wheels along the fence and a faux steer head atop the entrance gate completed the Western theme. (Courtesy of Sangamon Valley Collection, Lincoln Library.)

Bill Shea (left) landed on Omaha Beach on D-day and then spent his life along Route 66. He opened a Texaco station on Peoria Road near the fairgrounds in 1947 and then moved a block away to a Marathon station in 1955. He turned the pumps off in 1982 and sold camper tops before retiring to preside over his huge display of memorabilia and to swap stories with visitors. Shea welcomed Route 66 travelers until moving to a nursing home in 2013. He died on December 14, 2013.

Brothers Joseph, Hugo, and John Boente opened their first station in Carlinville in 1929, and the fourth generation of the family now runs 12 stations. Hugo Boente ran this station at Ninth Street and North Grand in Springfield. The Sangamo Electric Complex in the background is now the headquarters for the Illinois Environmental Protection Agency. A McDonald's occupies the service station site today. (Courtesy of Sangamon Valley Collection, Lincoln Library.)

Tony Crifasi, known for drawing caricatures of his customers, bought the Anchor Inn at 620 North Ninth Street in 1949 and changed the name to Stevie's Latin Village. It became one of the premiere dining spots in Springfield, popular with celebrities and tourists. The restaurant closed in 1972, and the building was demolished in 2009. (Courtesy of Sangamon Valley Collection, Lincoln Library.)

The Georgian Restaurant, operated by Joe Gerzin, opened in 1941 on the southwest corner of South Ninth Street and East South Grand Avenue. Soon after being hired as a waitress in April 1958, Mary Jane Hanselman, 16, disappeared after her shift one night. Her body was found a few days later and, although a cook at the Georgian was arrested, the case remains unsolved. The restaurant closed in 1986, and the building was demolished in 2005.

This winter scene on Sixth Street, in a view looking south toward Broad Place and the Wabash Railroad viaduct, was captured before Sixth Street through downtown became northbound only. Southbound traffic was moved to Fifth Street in 1949. In 1968, Sixth Street became one-way from North Grand Avenue to Stanford Avenue. (Courtesy of Sangamon Valley Collection, Lincoln Library.)

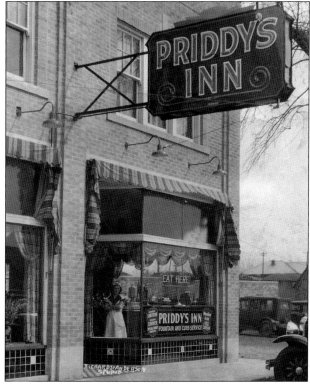

During the heyday of Route 66, a photographer for Anderson Studios captured a waitress looking out the window at Priddy's Inn, 2244 South Sixth Street. Priddy's developed into the Black Angus Steak House, in business from 1953 to 1983 and operated by Gene and Aida Petrili. It later became Jim's Steak House, then Gallagher's, and Charlie R's. (Courtesy of Sangamon Valley Collection, Lincoln Library.)

The Bel-Aire Manor at 2636 South Sixth Street was one of the finest and most modern motels in Springfield. Over the past several years, it has become long-term rentals and deteriorated into a crime-ridden haven for transients. As of 2014, plans for the city to purchase the property and turn it into a Route 66 Museum had stalled due to a lack of funds. (Courtesy of Sangamon Valley Collection, Lincoln Library.)

A. LINCOLN TOURIST COURT — U. S. 66 — SOUTH LIMITS OF SPRINGFIELD, ILLINOIS

Mr. and Mrs. William D. Posegate lived in the home next to their A. Lincoln Motel. It opened in 1947 with 24 units, plus some guest rooms in the house. The home gave way to a more modern office, and 18 more units and a swimming pool were added in the 1950s. The A. Lincoln Motel was demolished, and the Cozy Dog moved to this site in 1996.

While stationed in Amarillo during World War II, Ed Waldmire Jr. and his friend Don Strand developed a battered and French-fried hot dog on a stick. In 1946, Waldmire began selling his "crusty curs" from a small shack on Route 66. His Cozy Dog Drive In opened on September 27, 1950. Waldmire's son Bob, a renowned Route 66 artist and free spirit, died in 2009. A Walgreens now occupies the original Cozy Dog site, and the restaurant moved next door. (Courtesy of Cozy Dog Drive In.)

The Allis-Chalmers Manufacturing Company was a major source of employment and a landmark along City Route 66 on the south side of Springfield from 1928 to 1985. The Springfield plant was originally the location of the Monarch Tractor Company. In the 1970s, the plant became Fiat-Allis. This company shut down for good in 1985, and the Park South business development was constructed on the site of the massive manufacturing plant. This photograph shows the assembly line in 1945. (Courtesy of Sangamon Valley Collection, Lincoln Library.)

Emilio Copp opened Copp's Corner, a grocery store and café just outside the Springfield city limits, in 1932. Special guests could press a buzzer at the bottom of the back stairs to gain access to the prostitutes and gambling on the second floor. After World War II, it was sold to Guido Manci, who converted it to the Curve Inn, which is still in business today. It is the only building of Copp's complex still standing. (Courtesy of Sangamon Valley Collection, Lincoln Library.)

Holiday Inn founder Kemmons Wilson cut the ribbon to open the Holiday Inn East on January 24, 1965. The motel originally had 120 guest rooms, a 24-hour coffee shop, a restaurant and lounge, banquet and meeting rooms that could accommodate up to 1,000 people, and a heated swimming pool. It is now the Route 66 Hotel and Convention Center. (Courtesy of Sangamon Valley Collection, Lincoln Library.)

The Southern View Motel was once owned by state senator George William Horsley. In 1971, he initially refused to sponsor funding for Sangamon State University, due to "radical activities" and "scandalous behavior." As an example, he cited a faculty member who did not remove a "floppy hat" at a meeting with women present. The university responded by celebrating Floppy Hat Day. The Southern View closed in 1999 and has been demolished.

This 1963 photograph looks south on the new Interstate 55 from the Route 66/Sixth Street on-ramp at the south end of Springfield. The segment labeled here as Hazel Dell Road eventually became Interstate 72 going west toward Jacksonville. The Hazel Dell Road segment initially went to Second Street and then ended. (Courtesy of Sangamon Valley Collection, Lincoln Library.)

The Inn of the Lamplighter opened in 1956 and received raves from AAA as an "exceptionally well run motel on impressively landscaped grounds." The Lamplighter had a "Secluded Outdoor" pool and the "Tropical Indoor" pool. It closed in 1980 after Interstate 55 cut it off from the highway; it then became the Lamplighter condominiums. (Courtesy of Sangamon Valley Collection, Lincoln Library.)

Beginning in 1930, Route 66 followed North Cotton Hill Road over Sugar Creek south of Springfield. The creek was dammed in 1933 to create Lake Springfield, and the South Sixth Street Bridge was constructed to carry Route 66. A new bridge for Interstate 55 opened in 1967. The 1930 pavement still leads through the woods here to disappear under the lake. (Courtesy of Sangamon Valley Collection, Lincoln Library.)

In 1940, Route 66 was rerouted over Thirty-first Street (now Dirksen Parkway) and Linn Avenue (Stevenson Drive). The Springfield Drive-In, seen here at center, opened in 1949 at Bypass 66 and Route 29. It could accommodate 800 cars, and the screen was billed as the world's largest, at 62 feet by 46 feet. The screen tower rose 76 feet off the ground. The theater was closed in 1984. (Courtesy of Sangamon Valley Collection, Lincoln Library.)

From 1947 to 1987, race fans enjoyed the action at Joe Shaheen's Springfield Speedway, near the intersection of Clearlake Avenue and North Dirksen Parkway. "Jungle Jim" Davison raced there, and then went on to open Jungle Jim's Café. The café on Peoria Road became known for its racing atmosphere and the Barbie doll suspended from a zip line above the diners. (Courtesy of Sangamon Valley Collection, Lincoln Library.)

The Caravan Motel was located at the bypass route and US 54. The "place with the friendly air" was operated by Mr. and Mrs. Ira Tosh. The eight-unit motel opened in 1953 and was later known as the Dirksen Inn. The building, which still stands, later housed a paving business. The old sign, now gone, was chosen as "Best in Springfield" by readers of the *Journal-Register* in 1985. (Courtesy of Sangamon Valley Collection, Lincoln Library.)

Tony and Opal Lauck opened the Fleetwood Restaurant on the North Thirty-first Street bypass route in January 1957. The restaurant could seat 300 and was known for its roasted chicken, which Tony also sold at a restaurant called Chic-a-Rama. Linda Lauck and her husband, John Howard, took over in 1979. The Fleetwood closed in 1993; only the old signposts remain.

Billboards on Route 66 promoted the Lincoln sites in Springfield. Abraham and Mary Todd Lincoln lived at Eighth and Jackson Streets from 1844 to 1861. It was the only home they ever owned. Lincoln's tomb is in Oak Ridge Cemetery, a few blocks off Peoria Road. The magnificent Abraham Lincoln Presidential Library and Museum is located on North Sixth Street. The men pictured are unidentified. (Courtesy of Sangamon Valley Collection, Lincoln Library.)

From 1926 to 1930, Route 66 zigzagged a narrow path through the fields along the original Illinois Route 4 between Springfield and Staunton. Segments such as this one, three miles south of Chatham, were paved in brick to create jobs in 1931, after the Route 66 designation had been removed. A precious 1.4-mile brick section can still be driven north of Auburn. (Courtesy of Illinois Department of Transportation.)

On June 24, 1921, Illinois lawmakers authorized the Department of Public Works and Buildings to hire "a sufficient number of State Highway Patrol Officers to enforce the motor vehicle laws." The force at first was primarily concerned with enforcing weight limits on the "hard roads." In 1926, this trooper pulled over a reckless driver in a 1923 REO on Illinois Route 4 south of Springfield. The motorcycle is a Henderson four-cylinder. (Courtesy of Illinois Department of Transportation.)

Auburn is one of a string of mining towns on original Route 66 south of Springfield. This view of the west side of the town square shows the H&H Confectionery and Cafe in the local Independent Order of Odd Fellows (IOOF) building. Those buildings are gone, along with most of the others on this block. Auburn was the hometown of pro baseball player Emil "Dutch" Leonard, who played for several major league teams beginning in 1933. (Courtesy of Sangamon Valley Collection, Lincoln Library.)

Seven

MACOUPIN AND MONTGOMERY COUNTIES

Original Route 66 enters Macoupin County at the outskirts of Virden, where a monument in the square honors those who died in the Virden Massacre. On October 12, 1898, guards on a train loaded with strikebreakers brought in by the Chicago-Virden Mining Company fired on striking miners. In the firefight, eight miners and four guards were killed. It was a turning point in labor history, as the miners eventually won recognition of their union.

Deck's Drug Store, at right behind the flag, was established in 1874. Bill and Bob Deck operated the pharmacy from 1960 until the early 2000s. Bob and Renae Ernst took over the property in 2007 and established Doc's Soda Fountain and Pharmacy Museum. The original 1929 soda fountain is still in operation. (Courtesy of Doc's Soda Fountain and Pharmacy Museum.)

The 1926–1930 route passed the "Million Dollar Courthouse" in Carlinville. It was designed by prominent architect Elijah E. Myers, who also designed the Macoupin County jail. When completed in 1870, it was the largest courthouse west of New York City, but it was dogged by scandal and outrage over the price tag. Judge Thaddeus Loomis and his associate, county clerk George Holliday, were at the helm of the building committee.

The Loomis House, which opened in 1870, was also built by the scandal-plagued duo of Loomis and Holliday. They faced more criticism for using limestone from the courthouse project for their hotel. Holliday disappeared, and Loomis lost the hotel. It became the St. George Hotel, which is said to be haunted. The upper three floors have been unused since the 1970s, but the ground-floor storefronts house several businesses, including the St. George Room tavern.

The view in this 1936 photograph looks north on Illinois Route 4 approaching Carlinville, where the landscape has been drastically altered. The road was raised considerably and realigned in the 1950s. The ruins of this bridge are now hidden in the brush.

The 1926–1930 alignment of Route 66 came right down Gillespie's main street. Coal mining provided area employment, and the community was enjoying a newly built downtown after a devastating 1905 fire that destroyed the business section. The Dippold Drug Store (left) was established in 1919, and the building has since served continuously as a pharmacy. (Courtesy of Gillespie Public Library.)

The Coliseum Ballroom in Benld boasted the biggest dance floor between Chicago and St. Louis. Stars like Duke Ellington, Ike and Tina Turner, and Ray Charles played here. Dominic Tarro opened the ballroom in 1924. Tarro was indicted for bootlegging and was about to turn state's evidence when his body was fished out of the Sangamon River in May 1930. Robbers murdered his daughter Joyce as she returned home with the night receipts in 1976. The landmark burned down on July 30, 2011. (Courtesy of Jim Marcacci.)

DeCamp Junction was a small coal-mining community and home to the Riddel Store, which became the Duda Tavern in 1931. Duda's offered tourist cabins, dancing, and gambling. On June 19, 1934, five gangsters held customers and employees at gunpoint while they made off with liquor, gaming devices, guns, and cash. Today, the historic roadhouse on the original Route 4 alignment is known as DeCamp Junction, owned and operated by Loran Kovaly and Jim and Patsy Moultrie. (Courtesy of Loran Kovaly.)

At Farmersville, Harry and Fred Hendricks sold their station with a residence on the second floor to Cecil and Dorothy Hamilton in 1926. In 1937, former speakeasy owners Art McAnarney and Martin Gorman took over, and the restaurant became Art's Fine Foods. It reopened after a fire in 1952 destroyed the second floor. McAnarney died in 1957 and the business passed to his sons Elmer and Joe. They constructed a motel in 1960. The Route 66 Association of Illinois restored the 1960 Art's sign in 2007, but the restaurant and motel are now closed.

Edward McGaughey Jr. and his brother Edward both served as chief petty officers on PT boats during World War II. They later operated the Roundup Motel, café, and service station at Farmersville. They offered both Texaco and Mobil products and a well-stocked gift shop. The motel originally had 13 units and later expanded to 17. (Courtesy of Illinois Department of Transportation.)

The Shrine of Our Lady of the Highways has watched over travelers since it was dedicated on October 25, 1959. Frances Marten donated the site on his farm near Raymond, and members of the local Catholic Youth Council erected the statue of Mary. Marten kept the shrine lit around the clock, and he was one of the original five members of the Route 66 Association of Illinois Hall of Fame. His sons Lee and Carl have maintained the shrine since Frances died in 2002.

Brothers Shirley and Ellis Varner were originally machinists and later turned to farming. In 1950, they bought farmland along the west side of Route 66 a couple miles north of Litchfield and built an 18-unit motel with an adjoining café and Standard station. They did all the construction work themselves. Vandie and Beulah O'Conner operated the café.

The Overhead was famous for its chicken in the basket. It was established by Charles A. Aikman and Truman L. Felts and opened on July 1, 1948. Felts sold his interest to Francis "Lum" Fleming two years later. The building, originally a downtown grocery store, moved to a site on Route 66 north of the Chicago, Burlington & Quincy Railroad overpass.

The Sky View in Litchfield is the last original drive-in theater still in operation on Route 66 in Illinois. The Frisina Amusement Company opened the Sky View in June 1950. It originally had a capacity of 750 cars and offered dancing on the patio in front of the snack bar. The Sky View was later owned by Mid America Theaters and is now operated by Norman Paul and his wife, Del. (Courtesy of David A. Jackson Collection.)

Mr. and Mrs. Arthur Large opened Skinny's Cafe in 1935. Their first building, which burned down in the early 1950s, was located on the older Litchfield route. In 1939, they erected a new building and added gas pumps. Later, they added a tavern and an addition to the restaurant. In the 1950s, it became a sales and auction house and is now Diamond's Trailer Sales. (Courtesy of David A. Jackson Collection.)

66 Hotel Court
U. S. Hwy. 66
Litchfield, Ill.
AAA
Recommended

Lorman and Dorothy Mansholt took a correspondence course in hotel management to get a bank loan to purchase the 66 Hotel Courts in Litchfield from the McBride family in 1963. They operated it until the mid-1980s. The 66 Hotel Courts was demolished in 1999, and the site became the Route 66 Car Wash. Some items from the motel are on display at the Holiday Inn Express in Litchfield.

In 1946, Lowell "Hydie" Orr tore down the original Saratoga Café at Litchfield, which had been built as the Sunset Inn in 1937 by Charles and Harold Morgan. Orr's New Saratoga Café was described as the most beautiful restaurant between St. Louis and Chicago. The exterior was covered in vitrolite, and the interior featured chrome and leather fixtures as well as seven murals depicting hunting scenes. (Courtesy of David A. Jackson Collection.)

In 1924, Greek immigrant Pete Adam opened the Ariston Cafe in Carlinville. The name is derived from the Greek *aristos*, or "best." Adam and partner Tom Cokinos relocated the Ariston to Litchfield in 1929. The current structure, on the other side of the highway, opened on July 5, 1935. Cokinos sold his interest in the Ariston in 1936 and went on to run the Blue Danube and the Ranch Inn. (Courtesy of Nick Adam.)

The Ariston added a new neon sign in the back when four-lane Route 66 opened behind the restaurant. Since 1966, Pete Adam's son Nick and Nick's wife, Demi, have continued to offer the traditional service expected of a family-owned-and-operated restaurant. Paul, eldest son of Demi and Nick, and his wife, Joy, joined the family business in 2004. (Courtesy of Nick Adam.)

Vic Suhling built his station across from the Ariston in 1957 and hired Harry Wagner as manager. The station later became Stewart's Deep Rock, but it was demolished in 1990. The Litchfield Museum and Route 66 Welcome Center opened here in 2011. The museum was the dream of Martha Jackson and Anne Jackson, widow and daughter, respectively, of longtime Litchfield newspaper editor David A. Jackson. The sign was restored in 2013. (Courtesy of Jim Thole.)

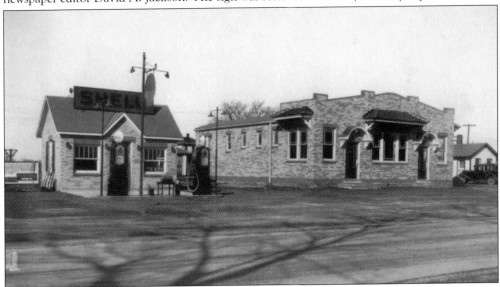

Albina and Vincenzo Cerolla opened a tiny gas station on Route 66 at Litchfield in 1929. By 1936, they had constructed a new home, a new station, a café, and a four-room motel. Their daughter Edith and her husband, Lester "Curly" Kradich, took over the Belvidere Café and Motel in 1950. The complex thrived until Interstate 55 opened. It is now mostly vacant. (Courtesy of Russell Olsen.)

Russell "Ruts" Brawley ran Rut's Corner Tourist Camp and Café, established in 1928. A larger tavern and restaurant, constructed after a 1936 fire, was known for its very busy slot machines. William Bahr ran the complex from 1947 to 1951 and then sold to the partners who constructed the Annex. The tavern is now Shaw's Club 66 Bar and Grill. (Courtesy of David A. Jackson Collection.)

Rut's Corner Tourist Camp was remodeled and reopened as the Annex in May 1951 by Joseph Roseman and Estell R. Felts, with Eugene Kozuk as manager. The complex included a gas station, and the ultramodern lobby and lounge was added in 1953. The Annex advertised itself as "on the airport beacon," as it was across from the airport runway. Only the motel units remain. (Courtesy of Sangamon Valley Collection, Lincoln Library.)

CC and Opal Simpson moved from the Subway Café to open the Gardens Café and Lounge in 1954. The bar was demolished after a 1963 fire, and a new motel opened in 1964. The Mansholt family bought the Gardens in 1978 and operated it until 2003. The motel became The Gardens–Best Value Inn, but the restaurant was demolished to make way for a Walgreens location.

Cemeteries refused to accept the bodies of the victims of the labor violence at Virden on October 12, 1898, so the miner's union established a cemetery at Mount Olive. Mary Harris "Mother" Jones, a crusader for the rights of workers and children who had played an important role in the strike, was buried here near the miners, whom she called "her boys," in 1930. A monument to the "Grandmother of all agitators" was dedicated on October 11, 1936.

Scherer's Café at Mount Olive, established in 1932, was open around the clock except for a month in 1942 when Route 66 was closed for repairs. The café made headlines in 1934 when a waitress thwarted an attempted robbery by firing a gas gun into the robber's face. The altered building later became Cruising 66 Bowling and Bar. (Courtesy of Steve Rider.)

Henry Soulsby and his son Russell opened a Shell station at Mount Olive in 1926, and it is now one of the oldest still standing on Route 66. Russell started a television repair business in the back of the building about 1949, and he ran the station with his sister Ola until 1993. The Soulsby Station Society and owner Mike Dragovich maintain the site today for Route 66 travelers.

The Joseph Roseman family opened the 66 Terminal two miles north of Staunton when the new four-lane highway was completed on the eve of World War II. A tall tower was added to attract the attention of passing motorists. When the motel first opened, there were no showers in the rooms. Patrons used a common shower building. The motel closed very soon after Interstate 55 opened. The building no longer stands.

This view of Staunton's Main Street looks west toward its intersection with Route 4 a few blocks away. Coal mining kept Staunton prosperous for many years, and the population peaked in the 1920s. Over the years, two other alignments of Route 66 zigzagged through town. Since 1989, Staunton has the been the home of the popular Tour De Donut bicycle race, which travels over 60 miles around the Route 66 communities of Benld, Gillespie, and Mount Olive.

Rich Henry, his wife Linda, and some furry friends greet visitors to Henry's Rabbit Ranch in Staunton. Volkswagen Rabbits are lined up nose-down in the ground in homage to the Cadillac Ranch in Amarillo, Texas. Rich Henry and his father, truck driver Hubert Henry, are in the Route 66 Association of Illinois Hall of Fame, along with Linda's father, farmer Wilton Rinkle. The Stanley Cour-Tel signs were salvaged from a suburban St. Louis motel slated for demolition.

Advertised as "halfway between Springfield and St. Louis," the Hi Café, Motel and Service Station opened in 1956 and took its name from the initials of owners Harold Hutchins and Frank Inthahar. It was open around the clock, advertising "25 hour service on US 66." The Hi Café held on for six months after Interstate 55 opened, closing in June 1977.

Eight

MADISON AND ST. CLAIR COUNTIES

The pre- and post-1930 alignments meet near Hamel, following today's Illinois 157. North of town is St. Paul Lutheran Church and its large blue neon cross. It was placed there during World War II by the Brunnworth family in memory of their son, who died at Anzio, Italy. The large cross has signified safe travels for those driving Route 66. (Courtesy of Greg Holmes.)

Much of the original alignment of Route 66 followed the Illinois Traction System, an interurban electric line that linked small towns across central Illinois with Peoria, Springfield, and St. Louis. The line became the Illinois Terminal Railroad in 1937. These Illinois Terminal cars, bedecked with a funeral wreath, are passing through Hamel on the last passenger run between Springfield and St. Louis in 1956. (Courtesy of Karen Wiesemeyer.)

George Cassens sold REO and then Hudson automobiles before he opened a Dodge-Plymouth dealership in Edwardsville and pioneered the use of trucks to haul cars. It started with his sons Arnold and Albert taking a bus to Detroit and each returning in a new vehicle towing another. Cassens Transport now operates 1,300 vehicle haulers nationwide. The cars are 1952 Packards. The tractor is a 1952 Dodge, and the trailer is an MHS Clipper. (Courtesy of Cassens Transport Company.)

George Cassens opened the Tourist Haven for his wife, Louise, to operate at the intersection of Route 66 and Illinois 140 in 1938. It was later known as the Village Inn, Earnie's, and then Scotty's. Today, the historic roadhouse is Weezy's Route 66 Bar and Grill, co-owned by Karen Wiesemeyer and Coleman Wiessman. (Courtesy of Karen Wiesemeyer.)

Edwardsville is the third-oldest city in Illinois and is named for territorial governor Ninian Edwards. At the time of this April 1939 photograph, taken on Vandalia Street, Route 66 through Edwardsville was being reconstructed with federal funds. Parts of the highway through town had originally been paved in brick, which was pulverized by the Madison Construction Company. (Courtesy of City of Edwardsville Historic Preservation Commission.)

In 1922, George Cathcart and his wife purchased the Joseph Hotz house at 454 East Vandalia Street in Edwardsville and opened it as a tourist home. Cathcart built a modest hamburger stand next door at 456 East Vandalia two years later. As business grew, he expanded the building to include a large restaurant and grocery. The café was open around the clock. Cathcart had a room next door and a bed in back so he could keep an eye on things. (Courtesy of June Nealy.)

The Hi-Way Tavern was established in 1934 by Frank and Dora Catalano as a combination tavern, café, and liquor store. It immediately became known for good home-cooked food and reasonable prices. The business was expanded in 1950 by adding on the house next door. Relatives George and Mary Lautner ran the expanded cafe. The building still stands. The van is a left-hand-drive Ford Thames, imported from the United Kingdom. (Courtesy of Joe Catalano.)

The Wildey Theatre in Edwardsville opened in 1909 as an opera house and second-floor meeting hall for the IOOF. In 1984, it closed as a full-time movie theater, but was purchased by the City of Edwardsville in 1999. Recently restored to its former glory, it is now in use for both concerts and movies. The dogsled in this 1927 photograph is a promotion for the movie *Wolf's Trail*, starring Edmund Cobb, Dixie Lamont, and Dynamite the Dog. (Courtesy of Joan Evers.)

The Edwardsville Garage was established about 1912. It relocated a few years later, and this building became Giese Motor Company, operated by Olin Giese. Albert Bothman established the first in a series of Ford dealerships to occupy the building in 1921. Giese went on to open the Oh-Gee Theatre nearby. Threatened by the competition, the owners of the rival Wildey Theatre hired him away. The Bank of Edwardsville occupies the garage site today. (Courtesy of Steve Rider.)

In 1927, Springer's Madison Oil Co. established a service station on the corner of St. Louis and West Streets, with Henry J. Springer Jr. as manager. Robert Smith and Ralph Ladd took over the station in 1936 and renamed it the West End Service Station. In the 1930s, a new building of yellow brick was constructed. It still stands today and has been occupied by a dental office since the 1960s. (Courtesy of Dr. Dale G. Claussen.)

From 1948 to 1964, Orval and Virginia Legate's Motel and Hilltop Restaurant were located on Route 66/St. Louis Road at the curve atop Sunset Hill. Patrons could catch their dinner in a big lake on the 12-acre grounds. Besides the 19-unit motel, an adjacent trailer park housed construction workers for the new Southern Illinois University Edwardsville campus. Highway realignment has drastically altered the landscape here, and no trace of the complex remains.

From Edwardsville, Route 66 originally followed St. Louis Road (now Illinois 157) to Chain of Rocks Road to Mitchell. That original route then followed Nameoki Road (Illinois 203) onto Madison Avenue in Granite City. The 1937–1954 alignment followed Nameoki Road to Edwardsville Road, past Earl and Gertrude Spalding's Auto Repair and Body Shop. Earl is seen here on the right gassing up a 1931 Ford. Check 'n Go occupies this site today. (Courtesy of Steve Rider.)

Industrialists Frederick G. and William Niedringhaus, makers of granite kitchen utensils, established the company town of Granite City in 1894. They built a massive stamping and enameling plant and also founded Granite City Steel. Thousands of immigrants and more industry followed. Several major industrial facilities still operate in the area today. (Courtesy of Central Electric Railfans Association.)

Original Route 66 crossed the Mississippi River on the McKinley Bridge, completed in 1910 and named for Congressman William B. McKinley. He ran the Illinois Traction Company, which built the bridge to carry its interurban trains. Automobile traffic originally ran on the outside of the trusses, and additional car traffic ran inside the trusses next to the trains. The McKinley Bridge was operated by the City of Venice for many years as a toll bridge and deteriorated until it was closed in 2001. An extensive rehabilitation was completed in 2007, and the McKinley now carries vehicle traffic while providing a vital link in a network of bicycle and pedestrian trails. (Courtesy of Central Electric Railfans Association.)

In January 1929, Route 66 was routed through East St. Louis across the Municipal Bridge. This bridge, the first free span over the Mississippi River at St. Louis, was completed in 1917. It was named for Gen. Douglas MacArthur in 1942 and closed to vehicle traffic in 1984. The bottom deck still carries rail traffic today. The bridge is shown here during clearance for the Jefferson National Expansion Memorial, which began in 1939.

East St. Louis was founded in 1799 by James Piggott, a Revolutionary War veteran who established a ferry crossing. It was the second-largest rail center in the nation by 1920. *Look* magazine and the National Municipal League named East St. Louis an All-America City in 1959, but industry was already moving out in search of cheaper labor and lower taxes. The combination of racial strife, corrupt government, and corporate greed turned East St. Louis into a symbol of urban blight.

This billboard, on St. Clair Avenue between Ninth and Tenth Streets in East St. Louis, welcomed travelers on US Routes 40, 50, and 66. At night, the sign was lit by incandescent light and ultraviolet, or black, light. The billboard was still standing in 2013, recently spruced up with a message proclaiming East St. Louis "The City of Champions." (Courtesy of Steve Rider.)

The railroad yards of East St. Louis were still bustling when this photograph with a west-facing view across the Mississippi River was taken in the 1950s. The Veteran's Bridge (right) opened in 1951 and carried Route 66 traffic from 1955 to 1967. It was renamed in honor of Dr. Martin Luther King in 1971. The famous Eads Bridge (left) opened in 1874, but it never carried US 66. (Courtesy of Missouri State Archives.)

As of January 1, 1936, the main line of Route 66 was rerouted to travel through Mitchell and across the Chain of Rocks Bridge. This route became Bypass 66 and 40 in 1955, when the main line was switched to the new four-lane highway (now Interstates 55/70) between Worden and US 40 near Troy. This bypass route was eliminated in 1965 after Interstate 270 opened.

The Bel-Air Drive-In at Mitchell opened in April 1954 and was in operation until 1987. During the 1970s, it had two screens, could accommodate 700 vehicles, and even featured a small indoor seating area with a big window. The drive-in is gone, but the marquee remains. The landmark is endangered, because the letters are falling off and the land around it is rapidly being developed.

Herman Raffaelle opened the Luna Cafe in Mitchell on September 1, 1932. Legend said that the cherry in the glass on the neon marquee was lit when the ladies were available, and that the Luna was a hangout for Al Capone. But restoration of the sign in 2012 revealed that the cherry could not be lit separately. Larry Wofford operates the landmark today.

Some motels with attractive signs were located at Route 66 and Illinois Route 3. The Chain of Rocks Motel was opened in 1957 by Bill and Barbara Thoelke. Bill once served as the president of the Illinois Hotel and Motel Association. The big sign came down in 2006. The Land of Lincoln Motel lost its sign in the early 2000s and became the Budget Motel. The Canal Motel was built by George W. Douglas and Robert G. Douglas in 1960 and is still in business.

The view in this 1952 photograph looks west from the newly constructed bridge that would carry the relocated Route 66 over the Chain of Rocks Canal. The eight-mile canal, constructed by the Army Corps of Engineers, opened in February 1953 and allows Mississippi River traffic to bypass a treacherous series of rock ledges known as the Chain of Rocks, on the northern edge of St. Louis. (Courtesy of Illinois Department of Transportation.)

The Chain of Rocks Bridge, shown here under construction, is known for its bend in the middle. The Corps of Engineers ordered the bend to prevent hindrance to river navigation. It opened in 1929 and carried Route 66 from 1936 to 1955 and Bypass 66 from 1955 to 1965. The bridge was originally painted silver, but the War Department ordered it painted olive drab in 1942 to appear less conspicuous from the air. (Courtesy of Steve Rider.)

This bridge carrying Interstate 270 over the Mississippi River opened on September 2, 1966, and traffic on the old Chain of Rocks Bridge slowed to a trickle. The old bridge was closed in 1970, and only a sudden drop in scrap metal prices saved it from demolition. It was used as a set in the film *Escape From New York* and was the scene of the horrific murders of Julie and Robin Kerry on April 4, 1991. Today, the old span is one of the longest pedestrian and bicycle bridges in the world. (Courtesy of Missouri State Archives.)

In July 1955, the Route 66 main line moved to the new four-lane highway (now Interstate 55/70) from Worden to US 40 west of Troy. From then until 1963, the two routes shared an alignment through Collinsville, the "Horseradish Capital of the World." Just south of Route 66 in Collinsville, the Brooks Catsup water tower is a roadside landmark. Completed in October 1949, it was narrowly saved from demolition and restored in 1995. (Courtesy of Mike Gassman.)

The Collinsville Road alignment passes through an area that was once home to the most sophisticated pre-Columbian civilization north of Mexico. Monks Mound, named for the Trappist monks who once farmed there, is the most prominent feature of the Cahokia Mounds State Historic Site. Monks Mound covers 14 acres and is about 100 feet tall. Cahokia Mounds was declared a UNESCO World Heritage Site in 1982. (Courtesy of Cahokia Mounds State Historic Site.)

Shown here on opening day in November 1967, the Poplar Street Bridge was the last Route 66 Mississippi River crossing. The route between Chicago, Illinois, and Joplin, Missouri, was decertified in 1974, but the shield signs remained up until January 1977, while work continued on Interstate 55 in Illinois. Here, the journey across Illinois ends, but ahead is the Gateway to the West and more adventure on Route 66. (Courtesy of Missouri State Archives.)

Discover Thousands of Local History Books Featuring Millions of Vintage Images

Arcadia Publishing, the leading local history publisher in the United States, is committed to making history accessible and meaningful through publishing books that celebrate and preserve the heritage of America's people and places.

Find more books like this at
www.arcadiapublishing.com

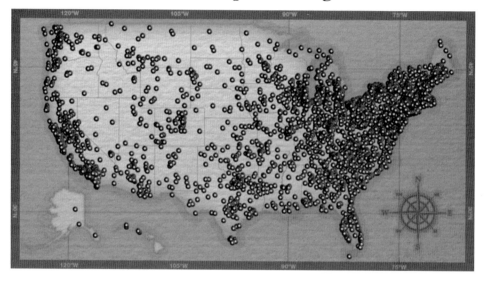

Search for your hometown history, your old stomping grounds, and even your favorite sports team.

Consistent with our mission to preserve history on a local level, this book was printed in South Carolina on American-made paper and manufactured entirely in the United States. Products carrying the accredited Forest Stewardship Council (FSC) label are printed on 100 percent FSC-certified paper.

MADE IN THE USA